Web
Entrepreneur

Walter Oleksy

the rosen publishing group's
rosen central
new york

With thanks to Adam Anderson for his help in writing this book.

Published in 2000 by The Rosen Publishing Group, Inc.
29 East 21st Street, New York, NY 10010

Library of Congress Cataloging-in-Publication Data

Oleksy, Walter G.
    Web entrepreneur / by Walter Oleksy
        p. cm. — (CoolCareers.com)
    Includes bibliographical references and index.
    Summary: Discusses what education and skills are needed to run a business on the Internet and profiles several successful Web entrepreneurs.
    ISBN 0-8239-3103-X
    1. Electronic commerce—Vocational guidance—Juvenile literature.
    2. Computer industry—Vocational guidance—Juvenile literature. [1. Electronic commerce—Vocational guidance. 2. Computer industry—Vocational guidance. 3. Vocational guidance.] I. Title. II. Series.
    HF5548.32.044 2000
    025.04'023'73—dc21   99-39012
                                                      CIP

Manufactured in the United States of America

17.95

CONTENTS

ABOUT THIS BOOK

Technology is changing all the time. Just a few years ago, hardly anyone who wasn't a hardcore technogeek had heard of the Internet or the World Wide Web. Computers and modems were way slower and less powerful. If you said "dot com," no one would have any idea what you meant. Hard to imagine, isn't it?

It is also hard to imagine how much more change and growth is possible in the world of technology. People who work in the field are busy imagining, planning, and working toward the future, but even they can't be sure how computers and the Internet will look and function by the time you are ready to start your career. This book is intended to give you an idea of what is out there now so that you can think about what interests you and how to find out more about it.

One thing is clear: Computer-related occupations will continue to increase in number and variety. The demand for qualified workers in these extremely cool fields is increasing all the time. So if you want to get a head start on the competition, or if you just like to fool around with computers, read on!

chapter one

THE WORLD OF E-COMMERCE

Do you use your computer to play games? How about surfing the Web for friends' home pages? Have you explored World Wide Web sites about your hobbies? Do you know how to research school assignments on the Internet, or how to send and receive e-mail?

If you know how to do most or all of those things or are learning how, you might consider a career working with computers. Many people who predict job trends say that's where the future is. Depending on your interests, you can choose among a wide range of computer careers. The more you know about how to use a computer, the better your chances of working in the area you like best.

Many careers in the computer industry involve cool stuff. Jobs that require working with computers include designing video games; combining sound and graphics to develop multimedia products; helping to create magazines, advertisements, or catalogs using desktop publishing; and designing Web sites for individuals and companies.

Working in the computer industry might be your ticket to success, as it has been for many. Even if you're not technologically talented or graphically gifted, you can pursue a career involving computers and the Internet. You might

You too may become a millionaire web entrepreneur!

even become a millionaire as a Web entrepreneur. That's someone who runs a business on the World Wide Web. Buying and selling goods and services on the Internet is called electronic commerce, or e-commerce.

Web entrepreneurs run their businesses at Web sites that are hooked into the Internet. People and companies order what they want from the entrepreneur's business and pay for it right on the Web, without even leaving their computers.

SO WHAT EXACTLY IS THE WEB, ANYWAY?

The World Wide Web—or just the Web, for short—is a part of the Internet, the worldwide computer network. You can think of it as a giant program that runs on the Internet in much the same way a word processing program runs on a computer's operating system. Unlike other Internet programs, the Web includes sounds and graphics (such as photographs and illustrations) as well as text.

To get to the Web, you use a Web browser. A browser is a software program that allows you to see and hear content on the Web. Netscape Navigator and Internet Explorer are the two most popular Web browsers.

When you open your Web browser, it takes you to a Web page. This page will contain information of its own as well as links to other pages and sites (collections of Web pages). The links are usually shown with colored text that is underlined, but they can also be reached by clicking on a photograph or other graphic element. The linked page may be part of the same site as the page you started with, or it may be at another site entirely. These links are created using HTML, or hypertext markup language, the main programming language of the Web.

According to *U.S. News and World Report,* more companies are doing business over the Internet every day. Some 80 percent of all Fortune 500 companies (the top 500 companies in the country, as ranked by *Fortune* magazine) were on-line in 1997, up from 34 percent the year before. International Data Corporation predicts that e-commerce will total $1 trillion by the year 2002. By 2008, people may do up to one-fourth of their shopping over the Internet.

People buy things on-line because it's more convenient than going to a store. It's convenient for companies to buy and sell things on-line too. They don't have to pay rent for a store, and they save money because purchases and sales are easier and take less time than they do in the real world. So more and more companies are looking for qualified people to help them carry out e-commerce over the World Wide Web.

Stories of people who have

It is convenient and easy to buy things on-line.

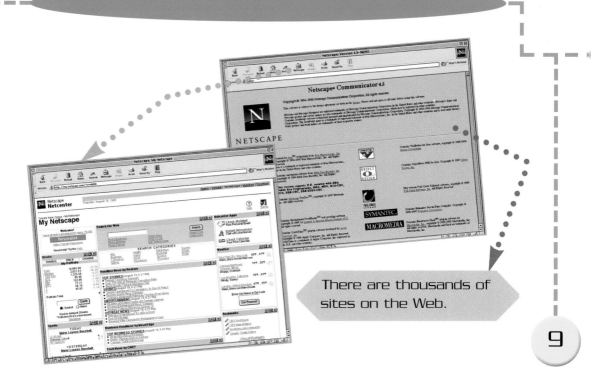

There are thousands of sites on the Web.

become multimillionaires working in the computer industry are legendary, and lots of those people exist. Some started their Web businesses while they were in high school.

Of course, there is no guarantee that you will become a millionaire as a Web entrepreneur. It usually takes a new idea (or a fresh approach to a not-so-new idea), some start-up money, and lots of hard work to make your Web business succeed.

In this book you will read about some successful Web entrepreneurs. If you work hard, study hard, and think creatively, you too might become a Web entrepreneur and develop your own cyberbusiness!

chapter two

A NEW WAY TO DO BUSINESS

Many people are so busy today that they don't even have time to go to the supermarket for groceries. Others are too rushed to go to a bookshop or music store and browse until they find the novel or CD that they want. Instead they surf the

Web and order what they need through Web entrepreneurs. An entrepreneur is someone who starts a business for

himself or herself. The word comes from the French verb meaning "to undertake." A Web entrepreneur is someone who conducts his or her business on the World Wide Web.

HOW E-COMMERCE WORKS ▶▶▶▶▶

People who are too busy to leave home and do their grocery shopping in a supermarket often shop by turning on their computers. They go to a Web site called Peapod.com. Shoppers check off the grocery items they want from a list on Peapod's Web page. Within an hour or so, after store clerks fill their orders, the bread, milk, and other items are delivered to the on-line shoppers' homes. This new way of doing business is called e-commerce, which is short for "electronic commerce."

Those who are too busy to buy a book or CD at a store can find time to shop on-line at Amazon.com or other Web sites that sell books, records, or videos over the Internet. Customers order what they want on-line and charge the items to their credit cards.

It often takes hundreds of people working in various parts of the country to fill the orders of Web entrepreneur businesses such as Peapod.com and Amazon.com. These people work in jobs ranging from order fillers, who get the desired items from the warehouse, to computer operators, who process and bill the orders.

Peapod is a popular example of e-commerce.

Peapod and Amazon were both started by people with new ideas about how to do business with computer technology. If you are good at selling, have a product or business many people want, and like spending time on a computer and surfing the Web, a career as a Web entrepreneur may be for you.

Web entrepreneurs aren't limited only to on-line shopping. In the following pages, you will learn about some of them. You will meet people who are making big money as Web entrepreneurs. Some of them began their on-line businesses when they were teenagers.

Why do so many businesses run by Web entrepreneurs have names that end in ".com"? That ending is part of a Web site's domain name, which tells the server you're using where to find the site on the Internet. Domain names for profit-making businesses end in .com for "commercial." Other common domain-name endings include "edu" (for educational sites such as universities), "org" (for sites belonging to organizations, usually nonprofit ones), and "gov" (for federal, state, and local government sites).

chapter three

WHO WEB ENTREPRENEURS ARE AND WHAT THEY DO

Most Web entrepreneurs have first gained some experience running or working for a real-world business. They may also have spent a lot of money to put their businesses on-line. But not always.

Aron Leifer of Brooklyn, New York, is a Web entrepreneur who started his on-line business with very little money. Now he owns property and stocks. He has a driver's license but prefers to pay a chauffeur to take him around New York City in his 1998 Infiniti Q45. Aron is only eighteen years old.

Aron is well on his way to becoming a millionaire Web entrepreneur through his computer software company, Multi Media Audiotext. He writes software programs for database management and computer telephone systems, and he serves clients around the

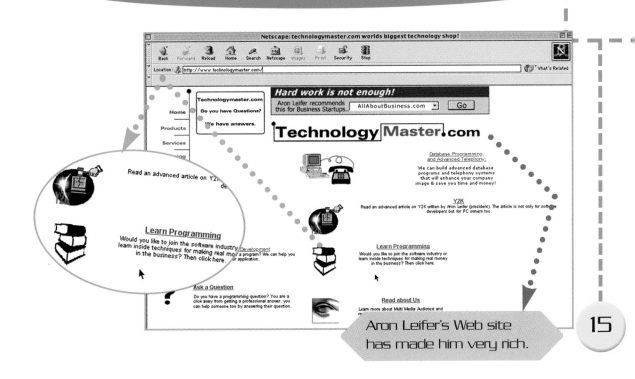

Netscape: technologymaster.com worlds biggest technology shop!

Back Forward Reload Home Search Netscape Images Print Security Stop

Location: http://www.technologymaster.com/   What's Related

Technologymaster.com

Do you have Questions?

We have answers.

Home

Products

Services

Hard work is not enough!

Aron Leifer recommends this for Business Startups.. AllAboutBusiness.com Go

Technology Master.com

Read an advanced article on Y2K de

Learn Programming

Would you like to join the software industry or learn inside techniques for making real money in the business? Then click here.

Development
We can help you
application.

Database Programming and Advanced Telephony:

We can build advanced database programs and telephony systems that will enhance your company image & save you time and money!

Y2K

Read an advanced article on Y2K written by Aron Leifer (president). The article is not only for software developers but for PC owners too.

Learn Programming

Would you like to join the software industry or learn inside techniques for making real money in the business? Then click here.

Ask a Question

Do you have a programming question? You are a click away from getting a professional answer, you can help someone too by answering their question.

Read about Us

Learn more about Multi Media Audiotext and

Aron Leifer's Web site has made him very rich.

15

world. At his Web site, *www.technologymaster.com,* he sells his software and tries to attract new customers.

Aron admits that before he started his Web business, he never earned a dime. He never even baby-sat or mowed lawns. He was too busy learning about doing business on a computer so that he could become a Web entrepreneur.

CAREERS IN WEB BUSINESS▶▶▶

Chances are, if you want to become a Web entrepreneur, you will first work for one at his or her Web-based company.

E-commerce Manager

Milan Vacval works for a Web entrepreneur company called the Vista Technology Group in St. Charles, Illinois, as an e-commerce manager. The company makes computer systems for food and packaged-goods companies and grocery stores.

Vacval prepared for work in on-line business by getting a master's degree in computer science. He applied for the job of e-commerce manager at Vista because, he says, "I've always dreamed of working for a software company."

His job involves developing electronic data interchange (EDI) systems for clients. EDI is an e-commerce tool that businesses use to transfer documents between systems. Vacval develops EDI programs to move data and information back and forth electronically among manufacturers, food brokers, and store owners.

"I enjoy the whole process of e-commerce," Vacval says. "It's exciting."

EDI systems allow e-commerce to work efficiently.

He is paid well to do the work he likes. The average salary for an e-commerce manager ranges from $70,000 to $100,000.

Vacval's advice to young Web entrepreneurs: "Keep your computer knowledge current.

Stay current with your computer knowledge.

Just because you're exposed to certain technologies doesn't mean you know all about them. You have to gain expertise in the ones you need."

A Web Business Team

Vacval is part of a team of people who make the company successful doing business on-line. The following are some of the positions (some requiring more computer skills and knowledge than others) that e-commerce team members may hold.

Web Site Producer/Associate Producer

🖰 What they do: Producers manage and direct the development of an Internet site for a Web-based business. Associate producers create the text and other content that appears on the Web site and keep the site up-to-date. They also work with sales staff on the design of the site and on advertising and promotion.

- Skills needed: Writing ability and/or graphic design skills, marketing skills and experience, and knowledge of Internet businesses. Some producer positions require writing experience and basic HTML skills. HTML is a programming language that creates links between different parts of a Web site and from one site to another.
- Salary: $30,000-$53,000

On-Line Marketer

Positions include brand manager, advertising sales coordinator, and account executive.

- What they do: You can't sell a product that no one knows about. That's where marketing comes in.

On-line marketers sell the company's products.

On-line marketers work with other departments to create advertisements and other ways to sell the company's products.

- 🖱 Skills needed: Research skills and/or a college degree in marketing or public relations.
- 🖱 Salary: $28,000-$60,000

Public Relations Associate or Manager

- 🖱 What they do: A public relations associate is the voice of the company. He or she works to make sure that buyers, investors, and businesspeople are aware of the company's activities. This person develops public relations plans, writes press releases, and keeps the media informed of the company's growth and success.
- 🖱 Skills needed: Communication skills, experience, and/or a college degree in marketing, promotions, advertising, or public relations.
- 🖱 Salary: $28,000-$60,000

On-Line Editor

- 🖱 What they do: On-line editors have duties like those of newspaper and magazine editors or TV and radio producers—they produce news. They are often involved in site production and design.

🖱 Skills needed: Writing skills and knowledge of current affairs or of the field that the company is involved in.

🖱 Salary: $29,000-$60,000

Others on the Team

Computer software designers, accountants, lawyers, customer support specialists, and consultants are among the other jobs that may be part of a Web business team.

According to the Internet site CareerBuilder Network, to succeed in the Web world, workers need to be creative and energetic. They must also be willing to work hard, put in lots of overtime, and deal with stress.

Nonetheless, the pay is good, and the work is interesting. It is one of the fastest-growing fields, with opportunities for those with high-tech skills as well as for non-techies. Working for an on-line business can lead you to success as a Web entrepreneur.

Web businesses often involve a lot of developmental teamwork.

chapter four

OCCUPATIONAL OUTLOOK

People who analyze businesses agree that the future looks bright for those working in computer technology. This includes Web entrepreneurs who offer new products or services on-line and those who work for them.

In a 1999 report, the United States Bureau of Labor Statistics listed computer technology among the top occupations in the nation. It reported that almost 250 different careers exist in computer technology. The industry is expected to grow 118 percent from 1996 to the year 2006. This means that more than twice as many people will be working

in computer technology at the end of that ten-year period as there were at the beginning.

THE FUTURE OF BUSINESS

Some of America's leading e-commerce entrepreneurs had a message for business owners at a meeting in Chicago in the spring of 1999: Every business, not just retail stores, had better get on board the Internet or be left in the dust. These business leaders point to the fact that doing business over the Web allows companies to do more work faster and also lets them reach more customers than they can in conventional ways.

More people are doing their shopping at Web-based businesses every day because more companies now conduct their business on-line. About 44 percent of U.S. companies sold products or services on-line in 1999, according to the Association of National Advertisers. Another 36 percent reported that they were planning to develop on-line Web sites in the next twelve months.

The average cost to develop a corporate Web site in 1999 was $252,000. Developing an e-commerce site—at which people can order products or services on-line—is more expensive because it requires more computer power and usually more workers. The average cost of maintaining an e-commerce site in 1999 was $369,000.

Those figures mean that companies spend a lot of money to do business on-line. But the payoff seems to be worth the investment. In 1998, for example, sales from on-line Christmas shopping reached a record $3.5 billion. That accounted for nearly half of the total on-line sales for that year.

Consumers like shopping on-line. "In the comfort of my own home, in the wee hours of the morning, I could shop to my heart's content," says Cathy Grayson Brower, editor-in-chief of *Small Business Computing* magazine. "Even toys that were hard to find in stores, like the Spice Girl Ginger, were a snap to locate shopping on-line."

Forrester Research, a business research firm, predicts that on-line sales will grow almost thirteen times in the next few years. E-commerce sales are expected to increase from about $7.8 billion in 1998 to $108 billion in the year 2003.

E-commerce sales are expected to increase dramatically in the near future.

chapter five

TRAINING REQUIRED

Most successful Web entrepreneurs get a good college education and then work in the computer industry. Only a very few have started successful computer businesses without such preparation. Students who think that they want to become Web entrepreneurs should plan to earn at least a bachelor's or master's degree in a specialized field such as business, marketing, or computer science. Also, it's very helpful to spend several years working in a Web-based business.

EQUIPMENT NEEDED ▶▶▶▶▶▶

A Web entrepreneur needs the following equipment:

- 🖱 A computer, with as much memory as possible and the fastest Internet connecting speed.

🖱 A way to connect the computer to the Internet. Traditionally people have used modems to connect to the Internet over a telephone line, but many Web entrepreneurs are taking advantage of newer technologies that provide faster Internet connections than even the fastest modems.

🖱 An Internet service provider that provides the Internet connection as well as e-mail service.

🖱 A fax machine, especially if the business does not offer customers the ability to order on-line. A fax machine may be built into the modem, but many business-people prefer a separate ("stand-alone") fax machine.

Web entrepreneurs need very specific equipment.

Equipment and technology are important to running a Web business. However, successful entrepreneurs say that knowing the answers to the following questions is even more important:

- 🖱 Whom are you selling to?
- 🖱 How will the customers know what you have to sell?
- 🖱 How can you prove that your product or service is better, or a better buy, than that of your competition?

Having and knowing how to use the right equipment can help provide the right answers to those questions.

HOW TO SET UP A WEB BUSINESS

Compared to starting a real-world company, it is usually not hard or expensive to put a business on-line. Small, simple Web businesses have been started in about fifteen minutes for just a few hundred dollars. All you really need to know are the basics of word processing and setting up a Web page. If you can type and

It does not require much money to start a simple on-line business.

click, you can do it! Most Internet providers offer free, easy-to-follow instructions on setting up a simple Web page. Although it's helpful to know HTML, Javascript, or other Web programming languages to create a sophisticated Web site, there is software available that helps users design attractive Web pages without being programming experts.

For a relatively small fee, you can also let professional services such as Yahoo Store set up your Web business. It adds to your expenses; it costs about $100 a month to sell up to fifty items. But you're relieved of a lot of time-consuming technical work and can concentrate on running your business and selling your product.

The best approach is to get to know people who are Web entrepreneurs already. If they have businesses that won't compete with yours, they may show you how they got started on-line.

If you decide to do it yourself, there are only a few basic steps to setting up shop on the Web:

1. Select an Internet service provider (ISP) that offers the most help to you and your business. Choose one that can help you design your business Web site and that offers on-line marketing advice. You may pay extra for these services, but it will be worth it.
2. Owners of storefront businesses make sure that

their windows are exciting and inviting. Do the same with your business "window," your Web site. Make it attractive but easy to read, and make sure it's simple to get to various links.

3. Make sure that your ordering and payment-processing system is easy to use on-line.

4. Take customer service seriously. If you have repeat customers and word of mouth recommendations, you'll get new and expanding business.

5. Market your site like crazy. Let potential customers know about it through e-mail campaigns and other promotions.

6. Change the look of your Web site regularly (at least once a month) to keep it fresh and exciting.

RULES FOR E-COMMERCE SUCCESS

It's not that easy to become a Web entrepreneur. Of all computer careers, it may be the hardest at which to be successful.

To be successful, always take your business seriously.

"A high proportion of e-commerce sites started by small businesses or individuals are unsuccessful," warns Gordon Whyte, an e-commerce analyst. "The main reasons are not paying enough attention to a few basic rules."

Rules for success in e-commerce include the following:

- Have something worth selling or provide a service people want and are comfortable buying on-line.
- Bring customers to your Web site. Marketing may be the difference between success and failure.
- Competition is intense, so create an outstanding Web site. It takes imaginative ideas to get people to use your site instead of going to those of other companies.
- Give complete shopping information on your Web site.
- Make it easy for customers to pay on-line.
- Provide first-rate customer service.
- Go international—sell to customers all over the world.

SUCCESS STORIES

A fascination with computers and an original idea have made many Web entrepreneurs rich. Meet a few of them now and see how they became successful in e-commerce.

THE MAN BEHIND NETSCAPE

Marc Andreessen became a multimillionaire at the age of twenty-six through being a Web entrepreneur. He cofounded Netscape Communications, which produces Netscape Navigator. Navigator is one of the most popular Web browsers. It is used by millions of computer owners who surf the Web.

Four years earlier, Andreessen was majoring in computer science at the University of Illinois. He began thinking of ways to make the Internet easier for people to use. He virtually revolutionized the field by writing the first program that let people browse the World Wide Web.

THE WIZARD OF ON-LINE SHOPPING

Jeff Bezos started an Internet-marketing revolution when he began his on-line business, Amazon.com. The simple idea of selling books from a World Wide Web site opened up unheard-of possibilities for shopping through a computer. Unlike a real-world bookstore, which has a limited amount of space, Amazon.com can offer any book that is in print. If a customer orders a book from Amazon.com, the company simply gets it from a distributor that carries that particular book, then ships it to the customer.

Bezos is an extraordinary Web entrepreneur because the business he started has inspired so many other on-line businesses. But he didn't start out as a computer whiz. In high school, he won a Florida science fair award for a project on the effect of zero gravity on the housefly. After graduating from college, Bezos worked on Wall Street in New York City. While playing computer games, he got the idea of selling books through the computer. He and five friends spent a year preparing before the bookstore went on-line in 1995.

Amazon.com quickly grew into a $20 billion on-line

business selling not only books but also music and videos. Bezos doesn't run his Web business alone, however. Some 1,100 employees fill 57,000 orders a day and keep track of customers' 6.2 million credit card numbers.

Although so far Amazon.com has cost more money to run than it has been able to earn, Bezos is one of the richest, sharpest, and most successful Web entrepreneurs around.

JAZZ LEGENDS AND WEB BUSINESS

Jeff Sedlik isn't exactly in the same league with Jeff Bezos or Marc Andreessen, and he isn't a millionaire. But he has fun and makes good money at the same time with his Web business.

Sedlik, a commercial photographer, was on his way to a photo session when the big idea for his company, Mason Editions, came to him. He decided to sell fine-art

Web businesses sell everything from books to art to medicine.

lithographs of great jazz musicians such as Cab Calloway and Dizzy Gillespie on his own Web business site. Less than three weeks after taking his business on-line, he had already made several thousand dollars. It had cost almost nothing for him to become a Web entrepreneur.

CHARITABLE WEB ENTREPRENEUR

Rick Lynch thought of a new way to get rich and support a worthy cause at the same time. In 1994, the Texas pharmacist became a Web entrepreneur by starting Fifty 50 Pharmacy. He sells products and medications on-line to people with diabetes.

Lynch chose Virtual Spin to set up his e-commerce business. It took him only one day and a few hundred dollars to take his pharmacy on-line. He has made so much money from his on-line business that he has donated $4.66 million to diabetes research.

Like Rick Lynch, many Web entrepreneurs have more ideas, energy, and ambition than they have money, at least to start with. They're usually very independent people; they'd rather work for themselves than for others. They are also willing to take risks and gamble with their futures. Some succeed, but many more do not. The on-line business world is not for everyone, and it is not an easy or guaranteed way to make a living.

chapter seven

LEARN TO BE A WEB ENTREPRENEUR

Some Web entrepreneurs have been successful despite dropping out of high school or college, but their numbers are few. Most get a college education, then work in the computer industry or at a job in which computers are applied to their field.

A 1999 federal study of salaries suggests that education pays. According to the study, college graduates with a master's degree earned an average of $63,229 a year. Those with a bachelor's degree earned $40,478, and high school graduates earned $22,895.

Marc Andreessen of Netscape Communications advises aspiring Web entrepreneurs to get a good education. He also says, "Get into the (computer) industry as rapidly as possible. Most of the interesting things are happening in companies, not at universities."

"Technology will be at the heart of any future career," says Andrew S. Grove. The chief executive of the Intel Corporation has two degrees in chemical engineering. His advice to college freshmen: "Use the next four years to build a foundation to make your way in a technology-infused world. Study as much of the exact sciences as you are capable of—math, statistics, biology—it doesn't really matter which one. All the sciences give you the logic you will need to lead a productive and remunerative (well-paying) existence for the next fifty years."

Bill Gates, chairman of the Microsoft Corporation and one of the richest men in the world because of the success of his computer software systems and programs, agrees. But he adds, choose a career that you really like. Says Gates, "People are best at the things they get very enthusiastic about." Jeff Sedlik is a good example of this. He took his passion for jazz and turned it into a successful on-line business.

Bill Gates is perhaps the most famous Web entrepreneur.

LEARN THE BASICS ▶▶▶▶▶▶▶▶▶▶

While you're studying math and science, you should also learn what a computer can do, especially with word processing, graphics, and the Internet. Learning programming languages such as HTML will be useful too, and before you learn those, you may find it helpful to learn simpler programming languages such as Visual Basic or C++. Take classes that will add to your knowledge of the latest computer technology. Best of all, create your own Web page about yourself or a hobby.

Math, computer, and science classes can prepare you for a web career.

Then see how easily you can turn it into a Web business page.

Just about any subject you might want to work in involves the use of computers. Learn that field of work and take any computer courses that relate to it. Business classes will also help you on the road to Web success.

Maybe you don't plan to go to college but still want to know more about computer technology. If that's the case, try checking into technical schools. Many of them offer courses in Web page design, programming, and other subjects that will help you learn to do business on-line.

Several organizations offer advice to young entrepreneurs:

- National Foundation for Teaching Entrepreneurship. Through camps, school programs, and teacher training, low-income students learn how to start a business.
- Rural Entrepreneurship Through Action Learning. Information about business ownership and management, primarily in rural areas.
- Junior Achievement. Offers programs taught by classroom volunteers from the business community and education about business and economics.
- Future Business Leaders of America (Phi Beta Lambda). Sponsors local organizations and national programs that teach students about business, government, and community work.

To find out how to contact these organizations, see Resources.Com in the back of this book.

GET E-COMMERCE HELP ON-LINE

If you want to learn more about what it takes to start your own business on-line, surf the Internet at the following Web sites. They help get Web businesses started and running. All of these sites offer at least some free information.

- Microsoft's FrontPage. Free on-line instruction in creating and managing small-business Web sites. Links include an on-line Web design workshop and a multimedia demonstration.
- Yahoo Store. The Web browser offers instruction in setting up a business Web page and serves as host for the finished site.
- iCat Commerce on-line. Boasts that "you can build a great-looking on-line store in fifteen minutes."
- NetObjects Fusion 4.0. Helps to build business Web sites. Download a free trial copy at *http://www.netobjects.com/free.*
- 3Com Small Office Solutions. A program from the 3Com Corporation that connects small businesses to the Internet.

Advice on Entrepreneurship

Some of the most successful young Web entrepreneurs

offer this advice to teenagers and preteens who may want to start their own on-line businesses someday:

- 🖱 Don't make earning money your main goal. Start a Web business that interests or excites you.
- 🖱 Be willing to work for little or no pay, at least to start. Offer what you have for free in order to get your business started.
- 🖱 Finish what you start. Don't give up.
- 🖱 Be a self-promoter. Tell everyone about your Web business. Post notices about it in stores and give out advertising about it.
- 🖱 Limit time spent watching television or other entertainments that take you away from your goal of becoming a Web entrepreneur.

So now you know how to become a Web entrepreneur. Is it for you?

Before you decide, perhaps you should click into a new Web site, *www.reconnecting.com.* It offers a directory of articles for "people looking to live a human life in a high-tech world."

This Web site helps us to think about the role technology plays or will play in our personal and work lives. It discusses ideas about how to preserve human values in a world that relies more and more on machines.

Reconnecting.com was founded by Tom Mahon, an author who has worked in computer technology for many years. He says that he does not mean to offer advice. His Web site tries to help people determine the role of technology in their personal and professional lives. This subject

Be a relentless self-promoter for your Web site!

is important to everyone who already works with computer technology or plans to do so in the future. It is especially important to young men and women who want to become Web entrepreneurs. They will be among the future leaders of the business world, who will have to face the changes and challenges of the twenty-first century.

WORDS.COM: GLOSSARY

cyberspace The imaginary "space" in which computers communicate with each other.

data Information that can be processed by a computer.

database A collection of data that stores, retrieves, organizes, and reports on data stored in a computer.

desktop publishing Creating text and/or graphics using a computer's word-processing capabilities.

digital A method of recording information electronically in numeric units.

e-commerce Electronic commerce, or business conducted over the Internet.

e-mail Messages sent electronically to and from different computers via a computer network.

entrepreneur Someone who starts and runs his or her own business.

graphics Photographs, illustrations, and other forms that represent objects without words.

hard drive Part of a computer system unit that stores the information put into the computer. A hard drive may be an external device attached to the computer or an internal part of the computer, but it is not easily removable, as a floppy disk is. Also called hard disk.

home page A person's or company's own site on the World Wide Web. Also, the first page of any Web site.

HTML Hypertext markup language: a programming language used to write Web pages and create links that allow a user to find more information.

Internet A global network of computers that are linked to each other over telephone lines and through other electronic means.

modem A computer accessory that translates data into tones sent over telephone lines so that users can send and receive text and graphics.

multimedia The combination of sound; visual elements such as graphics, animation, and movies; and text in one onscreen computer application.

network A group of computers connected so that they can all communicate with each other.

on-line To be connected to the Internet.

program The list of instructions that tell a computer how to complete a task.

software Programs that run on a computer and allow the user to perform various tasks on that computer.

surfing Using the Internet, particularly the World Wide Web.

World Wide Web The part of the Internet that contains graphics and sound as well as text.

RESOURCES.COM: ORGANIZATIONS & WEB SITES

Future Business Leaders of America (Phi Beta Lambda)
1912 Association Drive
Reston, VA 20191-1591
Phone: (800) 325-2946 or (703) 860-3334
Fax: (703) 758-0749
e-mail: general@fbla.org
Web site: http://www.fbla-pbl.org

Junior Achievement
One Education Way
Colorado Springs, CO 80906
e-mail: jawebmaster@ja.org
Web site: http://www.ja.org

National Foundation for Teaching Entrepreneurship
120 Wall Street, 29th Floor
New York, NY 10005

Phone: (212) 232-3333
Fax: (212) 232-2244
e-mail: nfte@msn.com
Web site: http://www.nfte.com

Rural Entrepreneurship Through Action Learning (REAL)
115 Market Street, Suite 320
Durham, NC 27701-3221
Phone: (919) 688-7325
Fax: (919) 682-7621
e-mail: ricklarson@realenterprises.org
Web site: http://www.realenterprises.org

WEB SITES

iCat Commerce Online
http://www.icat.com

How to Succeed in Electronic Commerce
http://www.ecommerce.miningco.com

3Com Small Business Connection
http://www.3com.com/smallbusiness/connection.html

Yahoo! Store
http://www.store.yahoo.com

BOOKS.COM:
FOR FURTHER READING

Ahmad, Nyla. *Cybersurfer: The Owl Internet Guide for Kids.* Buffalo, NY: Firefly Books, 1996.

AIT Kauffman Foundation Staff. *The "E" and Me Student Guide: The Entrepreneur in You.* Bloomington, IN: Agency for Instructional Technology, 1998.

Erlbach, Arlene. *The Kids' Business Book.* Minneapolis, MN: Lerner Publications Co., 1998.

Franchetti, Richard F. *How to Prepare for a Career in Business: Tips Students Can Use Today for a Successful Business Career Tomorrow!* Plano, TX: Portrait Press, 1997.

Fulton, Michael. *Exploring Careers in Cyberspace.* New York, NY: Rosen Publishing Group, 1998.

Henderson, Harry. *The Internet.* San Diego, CA: Lucent Books, 1998.

Hinshaw, Donna M. *Internet-Enable Your Cash Flow: How to Build a Web Site for Small Business Owners.* San Francisco, CA: Pelican Associates, 1999.

Horton, Joseph H., and John Raye. *The ABCs of Starting Your Own Business.* Lewisville, NC: Horton Publishing, 1994.

Ianarelli, Cynthia, and Wendy J. Peters. *The Adventure to Entrepreneurship: A Journey to Self-Discovery for Young Women.* Greensburg, PA: National Education Center for Women in Business, n.d.

McWhorter, Abner. *An Introduction to Business for African-American Youth.* Detroit, MI: Xpression Publishing, 1995.

Pedersen, Ted, and Francis Moss. *Internet for Beginners.* New York: Putnam Publishing Group, 1997.

Reeves, Diane L., and Peter Kent. *Career Ideas for Kids Who Like Computers.* New York: Facts on File, 1998.

INDEX

ABOUT THE AUTHOR

Walter Oleksy is a former *Chicago Tribune* reporter and editor. A free-lance writer, he writes novels and nonfiction books for adults, teenagers, and preteens. His books include *Lincoln's Unknown Private Life, The Information Revolution,* and biographies of Christopher Reeve, Princess Diana, James Dean, Leonardo DiCaprio, and Chris Farley. He lives in a Chicago suburb with his black Lab, Max, who likes to fetch tennis balls and talk.

PHOTO CREDITS

Cover photo © Superstock; pp. 6, 8, 16, 17, 23, 25, 26, 28, 36, 40 by Thaddeus Harden; p. 10 © CORBIS/Randy Faris; p. 18 by Shalhevet Moshe; p. 20 © International Stock; p. 35 © CORBIS/Judy Griesedieck.

DESIGN AND LAYOUT

Annie O'Donnell